Words of
FREEDOM

CHRIST SETS US FREE

Let us praise God for his glorious grace, for the free gift he gave us in his dear Son! For by the death of Christ we are set free, that is, our sins are forgiven. How great is the grace of God, which he gave to us in such large measure!

EPHESIANS 1:6–8

REJOICE!

The people who walked in darkness have seen a
great light.
They lived in a land of shadows, but now light is
shining on them.
You have given them great joy, Lord; you have
made them happy.
They rejoice in what you have done,
as people rejoice when they harvest their corn
or when they divide captured wealth.
For you have broken the yoke that burdened
them
and the rod that beat their shoulders.

ISAIAH 9:2–4

Words of
FREEDOM

Copyright © 1980 Lion Publishing

Published by
Lion Publishing, Icknield Way, Tring, Herts, England
ISBN 0 85648 257 9 (casebound)
ISBN 0 85648 293 5 (paperback)
Albatross Books, P.O. Box 320, Sutherland,
N.S.W. 2232, Australia
ISBN 0 86760 208 2

First edition 1980

Photographs by Robin Bath, pages 13, 23; Bruce
Coleman Limited: Eric Crichton, page 9; Frederick
Determann, page 37; Fritz Fankhauser, page 39; Sonia
Halliday Photographs: F.H.C. Birch, page 27, Sonia
Halliday, page 21, Jane Taylor, page 15; Lion
Publishing: David Alexander, pages 11, 43, Jon
Willcocks, pages 17, 29, 33, 35, 41, 45; Claire Schwob,
page 7; Scottish Tourist Board, page 19; Tear Fund,
pages 25, 31

Quotations from Good News Bible, copyright 1966, 1971
and 1976 American Bible Society; published by Bible
Societies/Collins.

Printed in Singapore by Tien Wah Press (PTE) Ltd

FREE FROM FEAR OF DEATH

It was only right that God, who creates and preserves all things, should make Jesus perfect through suffering, in order to bring many sons to share his glory. For Jesus is the one who leads them to salvation.

He purifies people from their sins, and both he and those who are made pure all have the same Father. That is why Jesus is not ashamed to call them his brothers . . .

Jesus himself became like them and shared their human nature. He did this so that through his death he might destroy the Devil, who has the power over death, and in this way set free those who were slaves all their lives because of their fear of death.

HEBREWS 2:10–11, 14–15

'LET HIM GO'

When Jesus arrived, he found that Lazarus had
been buried four days before . . .

Jesus went to the tomb, which was a cave with a
stone placed at the entrance. 'Take the stone
away!' Jesus ordered . . .

They took the stone away. Jesus looked up and
said, 'I thank you, Father, that you listen to me.
I know that you always listen to me, but I say this
for the sake of the people here, so that they will
believe that you sent me.' After he had said this,
he called out in a loud voice, 'Lazarus, come out!'
He came out, his hands and feet wrapped in
grave clothes, and with a cloth round his face.
'Untie him,' Jesus told them,
'and let him go.'

JOHN 11:17, 38–39, 41–44

SLAVES NO LONGER

God spoke to Moses and said, 'I am the Lord.
I appeared to Abraham, to Isaac, and to Jacob as
Almighty God, but I did not make myself known
to them by my holy name, the Lord. I also made
my covenant with them, promising to give them
the land of Canaan, the land in which they had
lived as foreigners. Now I have heard the
groaning of the Israelites, whom the Egyptians
have enslaved, and I have remembered my
covenant. So tell the Israelites that I say to them,
"I am the Lord; I will rescue you and set you free
from your slavery to the Egyptians. I will raise
my mighty arm to bring terrible punishment
upon them, and I will save you. I will make you
my own people, and I will be your God. You will
know that I am the Lord your God when I set
you free from slavery in Egypt."'

EXODUS 6:2–7

14

Then Moses and the Israelites sang this song to
the Lord:
'I will sing to the Lord, because he has won a
glorious victory;
he has thrown the horses and their riders into the
sea.
The Lord is my strong defender;
he is the one who has saved me . . .

'Lord, who among the gods is like you?
Who is like you, wonderful in holiness?
Who can work miracles and mighty acts like
yours?
You stretched out your right hand,
and the earth swallowed our enemies . . .

'They see your strength, O Lord,
and stand helpless with fear until your people
have marched past –
the people you set free from slavery.
You bring them in and plant them on your
mountain,
the place that you, Lord, have chosen for your
home,
the Temple that you yourself have built.
You, Lord, will be king for ever and ever.'

EXODUS 15:1–2, 11–12, 16–18

Freedom is what we have – Christ has set us free!
Stand, then, as free people, and do not allow
yourselves to become slaves again.

GALATIANS 5:1

You are the chosen race, the King's priests, the holy nation, God's own people, chosen to proclaim the wonderful acts of God, who called you out of darkness into his own marvellous light.

1 PETER 2:9

CREATION SET FREE

All of creation waits with eager longing for God
to reveal his sons.
For creation was condemned to lose its purpose,
not of its own will, but because God willed it to
be so. Yet there was the hope that creation itself
would one day be set free from its slavery to
decay and would share the glorious freedom of
the children of God.

ROMANS 8:19–21

GOOD NEWS

The Sovereign Lord has filled me with his spirit.
He has chosen me and sent me
To bring good news to the poor,
To heal the broken-hearted,
To announce release to captives
And freedom to those in prison.
He has sent me to proclaim
That the time has come
When the Lord will save his people
And defeat their enemies.
He has sent me to comfort all who mourn,
To give to those who mourn in Zion
Joy and gladness instead of grief,
A song of praise instead of sorrow.
They will be like trees
That the Lord himself has planted.
They will all do what is right,
And God will be praised for what he has done.

ISAIAH 61:1–3

IN THE NAME OF JESUS

One day Peter and John went to the Temple at
three o'clock in the afternoon, the hour for
prayer. There at the Beautiful Gate, as it was
called, was a man who had been lame all his life.
Every day he was carried to the gate to beg for
money from the people who were going into the
Temple . . .

Peter said to him, 'I have no money at all, but I
give you what I have: in the name of Jesus Christ
of Nazareth I order you to get up and walk!'
Then he took him by his right hand and helped
him up. At once the man's feet and ankles
became strong; he jumped up, stood on his feet,
and started walking around. Then he went into
the Temple with them, walking and jumping and
praising God.

ACTS 3:1–2, 6–8

THE TRUTH SETS YOU FREE

Jesus said to those who believed in him, 'If you obey my teaching, you are really my disciples; you will know the truth, and the truth will set you free.'

JOHN 8:31–32

Love your enemies, do good to those who hate you, bless those who curse you, and pray for those who ill-treat you. If anyone hits you on one cheek, let him hit the other one too; if someone takes your coat, let him have your shirt as well. Give to everyone who asks you for something, and when someone takes what is yours, do not ask for it back. Do for others just what you want them to do for you.

LUKE 6:27–31

THE SPIRIT OF FREEDOM

For the Spirit that God has given us does not make us timid; instead, his Spirit fills us with power, love, and self-control.

The Spirit produces love, joy, peace, patience, kindness, goodness, faithfulness, humility, and self-control.
There is no law against such things as these.

Where the Spirit of the Lord is present, there is freedom.

2 TIMOTHY 1:7; GALATIANS 5:22,23;
2 CORINTHIANS 3:17

RELEASED

Jesus went to Capernaum, a town in Galilee, where he taught the people on the Sabbath. They were all amazed at the way he taught, because he spoke with authority. In the synagogue was a man who had the spirit of an evil demon in him; he screamed out in a loud voice, 'Ah! What do you want with us, Jesus of Nazareth? Are you here to destroy us? I know who you are: you are God's holy messenger!'

Jesus ordered the spirit, 'Be quiet and come out of the man!' The demon threw the man down in front of them and went out of him without doing him any harm.

The people were all amazed and said to one another, 'What kind of words are these? With authority and power this man gives orders to the evil spirits, and they come out!' And the report about Jesus spread everywhere in that region.

LUKE 4:31–37

Some were living in gloom and darkness,
prisoners suffering in chains,
because they had rebelled against the commands
of Almighty God
and had rejected his instructions.
They were worn out from hard work;
they would fall down, and no one would help.
Then in their trouble they called to the Lord,
and he saved them from their distress.
He brought them out of their gloom and darkness
and broke their chains in pieces.
They must thank the Lord for his constant love,
for the wonderful things he did for them.

PSALMS 107:10–15

PERFECT FREEDOM

I will always obey your law,
for ever and ever.
I will live in perfect freedom,
because I try to obey your teachings.

PSALMS 119:44–45

Thanks be to God! For though at one time you were slaves to sin, you have obeyed with all your heart the truths found in the teaching you received . . .

Now you have been set free from sin and are the slaves of God. Your gain is a life fully dedicated to him, and the result is eternal life. For sin pays its wage – death; but God's free gift is eternal life in union with Christ Jesus our Lord.

ROMANS 6:17, 22–23

NOT GUILTY

There is no condemnation now for those who live
in union with Christ Jesus.

ROMANS 8:1

May the God who gives us peace make you holy in every way and keep your whole being – spirit, soul, and body – free from every fault at the coming of our Lord Jesus Christ.

1 THESSALONIANS 5:23